Table of Contents

Introduction

Chapter 1: Facilities for Creating A Podcast

  1.1 Apps for Digital Recording for Podcasting

  1.2 Podcast Recording for Cell Phone

  1.3 Microphones

  1.4 App Podcasting

  1.5 Your Podcast Recording

  1.6 Environment

Chapter 2: Techniques for Podcasting

  2.1 Edit Your Podcast

  2.2 Your Completed Podcast export

  2.3 Podcast Hosting

  2.4 Being Mentioned in Your Podcast

  2.5 Niche Directories

Chapter 3: Availability to Your Audience

  3.1 How to Work Podcast

  3.2 The Secret Sauce of Podcasting

  3.3 Dedicated Authoring Tools for RSS Feeds

  3.4 Your Podcast Finds A Home

  3.5 Managing A Website of Your Own

  3.6 Your Domain Registration

Chapter 4: Distributing Your Media File

  4.1 Using Your Web Server

  4.2 Use a Hosting Service Podcast

  4.3 Use A Network for Content Delivery

  4.4 Using Sharing from Peer-To-Peer

Chapter 5: The Business of Podcasting

  5.1 Comprehension of Expenses Before Gains

  5.2 The Hosting Realities

  5.3 Learning the Fundamentals

  5.4 Advertising Costs Money

  5.5 Making Fair Use Feasible and Machine-Readable

  5.6 Licensing

Chapter 6: Money Making with Podcasting

  6.1 Make Money from The Media

  6.2 Contributions and Subscriptions

6.3 Promotion as a tool

Conclusion

References

Introduction

The word "podcasting" was not invented until a short while later, but the concept remains the same: if you have a post, use easy software and cheap equipment to record it and then publish it for the world to hear on the Internet. We have listeners on every continent and get input from all over the world, and we do it all from our Wisconsin farmhouse's living room, even in our pajamas.

Perhaps when the term "podcasting" came up, you were casually surfing the Web or scanning your newspaper. The phrase has slowly popped up again and again, like a building wave that would make champion surfers salivate with joy, and your interest continues to pique as the word "podcasting" echoes in your ears and persists as a riddle wrapped in an enigma in the back of your mind, super-sized with a side of fries and a diet soda to go. This book will take you through the Internet's fastest-growing technological revolution. The fundamentals will be in place by the time you hit the end of this book to get you, your voice, and your message heard around the world, and you can even have a bit of fun along the way.

Podcasting can be achieved on a range of budgets, from recording to web hosting, ranging from frugal to Fortune 500. You can podcast anything, including podcasting for its own sake, literally. As blogging has given a voice in politics, religion, and daily life to the anonymous, the famous, the "almost-famous," and the "used-to-be famous," podcasting adds volume and tone to that voice. Words on a website are frequently misconstrued because the hidden meanings and observations concealed within the text are hard to capture. But when those words are actually spoken aloud, when the message is sent, the interpretation of the sender is straightforward, succinct, and leaves no room for doubt. To many individuals, podcasting is many things, but it's a remarkably easy and effective technology at its most basic. What it means boils down to one individual: you. Some equate it to the radio (online radio at least), but it can do, and be, so much more. Podcasting is a modern communication medium that transmits the voice and its message across the globe without using public airwaves, linking the Global Village in ways that the Internet, RSS, and MP3 compression makers would probably never have thought of. It is the special and hard-to-find material on commercial, college, or public access radio that cannot find a location. You're about to embark on a thrilling journey into undiscovered land, and you'll find out here that all these kinds of stuff are podcasting and so much more.

There will be plenty of answers on these pages, and if you find our answers too easy, we will give you plenty of studies on your own time reference points. We wouldn't say that we have all the answers, quick fixes, and resolutions for all possible questions for podcasting, but we present the basic building blocks and first steps for starting a podcast to you. Our duty, as with this book, is to give you the base on which to build. That's what we did our best to achieve: send you the enchanted stuff that makes a podcast possible. This book was written as a linear route from conceptualization phases to your work's final publication. Not everybody wants to read the book from page one, however. Jump around from section to section and read the bits you need if you've already had your feet wet with the different aspects of podcasting. For when the going gets murky, we have plenty of guides back to other related chapters.

Podcasts can be either audio or video, as you have picked up by now. They are most often in an audio format, simply because it is the best way to record them, and it makes them easy to use as you can listen to them on your MP3 player on the go. However, several individuals film a video series, more like a TV series, and release it as a podcast.

Podcasts are mostly very similar to radio shows when you listen to them. Each podcast will have a specific theme: mountain biking or knitting, for example. In this topic, each podcast episode will talk about a specific topic: for example, how to knit a scarf or how to jump your bike. Normally, you'll have either one or a few presenters talking about that subject, but then you'll hear guest interviews. Most podcasts are really easy-only a few friends talking about a topic-and they are great and really easy to produce. Some of the more professional podcasts are made, however, such as radio and TV shows. Theme music at the beginning, background music during the podcasts, and little sound effects between interviews or parts may be used. They sound fantastic, but the production takes a lot longer.

One of the things about podcasts that people find most confusing is how they vary from standard audio or video files. Oh, at the same time, it's both pretty straightforward and a little complicated. The easy response is that an episode of a podcast is only an audio file you can subscribe to. This is achieved by a technology called RSS (the complicated bit...); however, the good news is, if you use a podcast hosting website, you don't need to think too much about the feed itself; it's managed for you. Basically, it means you have a list of podcasts that you have subscribed to, and when they're published, new episodes of those podcasts automatically appear on your screen. You'd have to check for them on the web with regular audio files and download them yourself, but RSS feeds allow you to do all of that. The key thing to note is, an audio file is just an audio file of its own. But an audio file posted to a website and included in an RSS feed to be listened to by individuals is a podcast!

There are a few different ways you can listen to a podcast, and some of them depend on how the podcast creators publish your podcast. Only navigate your way to the website on which it is hosted, find the episode you want to listen to, and click the play button is the best way to listen to a podcast. It's that! For this process, all you need is a PC or a Mac and an internet connection. The majority of podcast websites will allow you to directly play the podcast episodes on the web page. But that obviously means that you're attached to your PC, which is not very versatile.

The best way to listen to a podcast is always to load it into a certain kind of MP3 player so that you can play it when you're out and about. This means somehow downloading the podcast from the website. The page that allows you to play the podcast would usually allow you to download it as well. So, you can download the podcast to your device, pass it to your player, whether it's an MP3 player, an iPod, or a cell phone, and instantly listen to it. You need a computer, internet access and a digital mp3 player (mobile phone, iPod, etc.) for this method. Automating your Podcast Listening, Of course, the most effective way to listen to a podcast is to use all the RSS feed capabilities to automate the whole process. This takes a little more setup and needs additional software, but if you listen to a lot of podcasts, and particularly if you want to keep up with the entire series, then, in the long run, it's the best way. You don't need to go this far sometimes, of course, and it's best to only download one here or there, but it's worth covering up.

You need special tools called podcatching to listen to a podcast. iTunes or Juice are examples of these, but there are a variety of choices out there. Many music players have added podcatching capabilities to their list of options, a good example being the winning amp. Most of these alternatives are free, so you don't have to spend a penny to get a podcast. As an instance of a podcatcher, let's take iTunes. Thanks to its fantastic podcast directory, which is included in the iTunes store, it is one of the most powerful examples. Plus, almost definitely, it's the most frequently used. You simply go to the iTunes Store to subscribe and type in the topic you're looking for in the search box.

Using a smartphone podcasting app is an alternative to computer-based apps. This implies that you have an application that handles all your podcast subscriptions on your phone or tablet. So, you never need to re-plug your system into your computer. A lot better! Apple has its own podcasting app that gives iTunes a good alternative. However, it also takes advantage of the iTunes store catalog because it has an impressive directory and is one of the best podcasting applications out there. However, if you have an Android computer, don't worry. On the Android platform, there are some excellent tools for podcasting. My favorite podcasting app and the one I use to manage my own podcasts is Beyond Pod. Currently, it has a lot more versatility and is much more effective than the Apple version. Anything if it's missing is a very detailed directory, depending on a slightly less efficient search. However, you can get around that by only searching on the web for your podcasts, or even using the iTunes store to browse, and then copying over the URL of the feed. Dogcatcher is another option, and there are a few more out there too. As a great Podcast distributor, Stitchery gets a special mention, and it has its own smartphone app. The directory is more restricted than most, but some excellent podcasts are hosted.

Chapter 1: Facilities for Creating A Podcast

So, whether it's via the iTunes store, the Beyond Pod quest, or otherwise, it is possible to automatically subscribe to a Podcast. Often, though, you won't be able to find the podcast you're looking for, no matter what site you're using. You have to manually connect a podcast to the player in this situation. This is done by copying the podcast RSS feed's web address (or URL) and pasting it into the podcatcher. All podcatchers will have a fairly prominent 'Add a Podcast' option. When selecting the RSS feed address, it will request it. By looking at the website and following links to 'Subscribe,' you will usually find the RSS feed address of a podcast. It's also promoted quite well. You can look for an RSS icon occasionally, which is seen here. You are usually taken to the RSS feed page after clicking the button. You can only copy the page's address from the browser's address bar and place it in the podcatcher. You'll be delighted to find out that it's extremely easy to make your own podcast, and it takes very little equipment. Perhaps better, you also already have the equipment you need. I'll go over exactly what you need to make your own podcast in this section and where you can go about finding it.

1.1 Apps for Digital Recording for Podcasting

A recording system is the most basic thing you need for any podcast. You naturally need to be able to record your voice in order to make an audio file! Recording equipment takes several types, from very basic Dictaphones to professional audio recorders of the maximum quality. Plus, your machine can serve as a recording device. Using little more than a laptop and its integrated microphone, it is easy to record a daily podcast. It's usually beneficial to have at least a basic mobile recording unit for good performance. Without a recorder that you can bring around for all your podcast making, you would be stuck on your computer desk, and, particularly with a community, that's sometimes not ideal. As the quality is very dependent on price, it's worth spending more than the minimum on a recording unit. In general, going past the £ 50 + mark brings you beyond the range of recorders of decent quality, and you can spend infinitely more than you try. This kind of specialist journalist-level kit sells for £ 300 or £ 400 and comes with all kinds of functions.

Only purchase what you can afford or use the equipment you already have available to get started. Better to get started than not at all with the simple kit! The H4n also enables you to record using professional-level microphones, providing two XLR links. Right now, you don't have to think too much about what that entails, but it's enough to assume that if you purchased this recorder, you wouldn't have to upgrade it until you switch to advanced recording and other equipment levels. Having said that, since it comes with an integrated preamp, you might also plump for its successor - the Zoom H5 - for around £ 200. As an introduction to the craft, the Hn4 is still fantastic and is £ 60 cheaper. If you ever get the chance, these are the journalist-level devices I described earlier and could be used to prepare a story for the BBC!

1.2 Podcast Recording for Cell Phone

If you don't want to spend some cash on podcasting, though, you might look at the equipment you already have. Cell phones are fantastic recording devices and given that they are designed exclusively for recording and transmitting your voice, it makes sense. Almost every smartphone would have a voice recording capability, and there are great recording and editing facilities for devices like the iPhone or Samsung Galaxy. They also allow you to automatically email the file to yourself, so you still have a backup in case you lose the computer. And if you don't have a smartphone, you can still function as a Dictaphone on many older phones. You could discover an audio recording or Dictaphone feature that you never knew you had by scrolling through your phone menu.

1.3 Microphones

If you have the money, one great addition to your podcasting kit list is an external microphone. Even a low-cost microphone can enormously enhance the ease and consistency of your recordings. You may take external mics from any of the above recorders and gain from using one. Saying that bear in mind that to enhance the H4n's internal offering, you will need a very good quality mic. You will almost probably need an external microphone if you are recording from a device. Normally, the microphones built into laptop PCs are very poor quality and not worth using. You have an immense number of choices for computer recording. The job will be pretty well done by a normal headset microphone-the kind you can use with Skype. A good quality recording is produced by Canyon headsets, available on Amazon for about £ 15. However, some headset mics can be very small, so it's worth sticking with the Canyon or finding a Microsoft Live chat mic for yourself. Another high-quality headset mic for just £ 20 to £ 30 is the Live talk. The downside to this Live Chat is that it's just about USB. That's great; if you're just planning to record through the machine, it makes it very easy to set up and does not depend on your audio settings. But, if you're out and about and want to plug in your recorder with an external microphone, you'll need the regular Canyon headphone jack. However, if you're looking for the next step up, as seen, you might go for the Samson Go Mic. This is another USB microphone and, for the price, produces excellent results. As it comes with an in-built mic clip, it's also very versatile, so you can stick it to almost anything and make it really easy to record with. If you're going to do a lot of work with your digital recorder outside the workplace, you may want to get a microphone that looks more conventional. The ATR 6250 audio technology is a relatively low-cost mic that plugs into any recorder with a tiny mic jack (same as your headphone socket), and if you pay a lot more than that, as long as it's from a good brand, you're generally guaranteed good quality. Microphones are surprisingly technical bits of kit, and there are all kinds of combinations and configurations, but when you first start out, you can get a decent one for less than £ 50, so don't think too much about the higher end ones. Sometimes, when it comes to final recording efficiency, it's more about the setting than the microphone.

Podcast microphones in our world are always a hotly debated topic. Everyone has a personal favorite of their own, and there's a lot of talk about what degree of quality you really need to run a good podcast. Lots of podcasts use resources such as Skype and Google Hangouts to record people in various places, so connection quality can be more critical than your microphone. Others record in-person, so the atmosphere and mic technique play a role. However, there's no doubt that a podcast captured on a good quality microphone is massively more professional than anyone blabbering away on a tinny microphone headset. We've gathered a list of the best podcasting microphones on the market today if you're looking to improve the efficiency of your package. Two different tiers, entry-level and high-end, are included. We don't go into the realms of pro mics because, lets be frank, you don't need us to tell you what to do if you have the expertise to make it possible for you to get the best out of that level of equipment! So, why invest in a microphone of decent quality? And it's the mic that has the greatest influence on your recording quality. The mic records the speech and converts it into digital bits and bytes from actual sound waves. It can cost hundreds of pounds to get a decent microphone, but fortunately for us, there are a few more affordable choices too.

I'm talking as great as anyone would want for podcasting up to 6 figure viewers when I say high quality. In this segment, the microphones are within the usual Budget of the Podcaster and provide great quality recordings to boot. The next step up is the professional level, such microphones that a professional recording studio will gladly kit out. But, be prepared for a serious cash outlay at that stage. The microphones in this section will do the job perfectly unless you're making a living off your podcast (and even if you are, really!).

The Podcaster is a dynamic podcast microphone that is simply outstanding. When you have stands and a shock mount, the price is certainly creeping up a little now, but if you compare it directly with one of the entry levels microphones above, you will find a big difference. Like the MXL990 below, this is an XLR microphone, but being dynamic, it doesn't need phantom control. That means that you can plug it with the right cable into a 1/4" jack just as easily as the XLR, so you have a little more versatility about how it can be used. Rode has also developed an in-built pop filter to help you with your plosives a little bit. If you want this quality standard, but without the extras, then it could be the perfect option for the Rode Podcaster. It's a high-quality USB microphone, a cut above the bottom of the Blue Yeti, but a price to reflect that, of course. Of course, for home recordings, the Rode Podcaster could be the best option because it's a dynamic microphone rather than a condenser. In noisier settings, dynamics have a major benefit.

If you want your podcast to have that extra degree of scope, it may be worth opting for a condenser microphone, but with some caveats. Condenser microphones work in a totally different, un-fathomable way, but it's enough to claim that they give your recordings a higher degree of quality. Nevertheless, and this is important, it only applies in the correct sense. The problem is condenser microphones appear to pick up a lot of background noise because of their sensitivity. This implies that to take advantage of the quality they provide; you need a good, quiet recording environment. They also seem to be much more delicate, so in your pack, they're not ideal for bringing around.

The other downside is that external power is required for condenser microphones. This usually comes from a phantom power source, either supplied by a mixing desk, your digital camera, or a microphone battery. Digital recorders or mixing desks themselves are good investments because they provide a lot of versatility, but that's also an additional investment. To be frank, mixers appear to be overkill for most podcasting setups. Essentially, in a very quiet setting, if you want the highest sound, but intend to only record from your desk, using a mic stand, then a condenser microphone might be perfect for you. The Samson C01 Studio Condenser Mic, from the same business, is a fine example of an entry-level condenser microphone. Of course, a Dynamic Microphone is an alternative. Essentially, dynamic mics are the opposite of anything I've mentioned above. They record a narrower frequency spectrum, and so they can sound a little less rich. They record less surrounding noise, so you need to be close to the microphone right away. But they can be lovely and silent and forgive even worse recording conditions because of both of those characteristics.

The two variables that decide which microphone you should go for are your budget your recording environment purchase a podcasting microphone as pricey as you can afford. The more you play, the higher the quality you will get, as with anything. This, however, only goes up to a degree. With the ATR2100, you'll get perfectly good results, so if that's your budget, then start here and step up. You can spend hundreds while upgrading, but to take advantage of the quality provided by something like the Shure SM7B, you need a lot of experience and more specialized support equipment. Save that when you've become an audio production guru for a few years down the road and stick with something like the Rode Podcaster or the Blue Yeti USB Microphone for now. The dynamic vs. condenser microphone problem comes down to where you usually record and how many kits you want to use. If you have a good, comfortable, daily recording space, then it might be worth buying a condenser microphone. You're not going to be able to take it easily anywhere, and you're going to need the mixer or digital recorder to provide the power unless you find a mic powered by a battery. But the depth of your recordings is going to be fantastic, and you're certainly going to stand out. Enjoy it, whatever you choose, and note that the key thing is to continue releasing those podcasts!

1.4 App Podcasting

You can actually create a podcast without any programmed at all in ideal circumstances. You could make a recording and instantly upload it, without editing, to your podcasting hosting room. This depends on your recording being pretty precise, of course, and making no slips or errors! In fact, individuals make mistakes, and before you publish it, you sometimes need to make edits to an audio file. You may also want to add music or sound effects to a podcast or stitch together two different audio files, such as your introduction and an interview you did at another time. You need audio editing tools in this situation. The good thing is the option is easy. If you don't already have an audio editing kit, then the package for you is Audacity. It is strong, and it does everything you need, and, best of all, it's free! On both Mac and PC, Audacity works, so you don't need to think about the platform. That's why it's the program I'm teaching, and that's what I'm covering in this book. It's free, it's versatile, it's accessible to everyone, and that counts for a lot. However, if you're on a Mac, a rather popular alternative is the Garage band. It's very simple to use, it's a strong piece of software, and best of all, it's free! The next up on the Audacity list on the PC will be Adobe Audition CC (Creative Cloud). This isn't a cheap little piece of software, but it's really fine. However, many individuals say. Audacity is just as strong, or even more so, so it can be difficult to justify the cost. However, if you use other Adobe apps, you may have Audition packed in, so it's worth a try in that case. No matter what you want, that's all we need to start recording!

1.5 Your Podcast Recording

It's time to grab a glass of water, warm up your voice, and record! We'll look at how to record your podcast in this chapter, including scripting and how to configure your recording room. This is the question posed by any future podcaster and one of the podcasting planning areas that is most discussed. Will a complete script be written? Fortunately, if not really helpful, the response is easy-it depends on what you are comfortable with! I know a lot of podcasters who barely write down anything. They know their subject back to front, and with a broad overview of what they're going to talk about, they just go into the recording. They may have 4 or 5 bullet points, and, smooth and polite, they come across great on air. This approach's spontaneous and unplanned nature makes the podcast sound very personal and engaging, and if well done, it can sound fantastic. It takes very little planning, too. Using this form, you can very easily create a podcast. The pitfall to this strategy is that you would sometimes stumble over your thoughts, run out of stuff to say, or simply fail to cover everything you wanted to cover without a script, expert or not. Doing a 20-minute podcast with only a very broad outline can be very challenging. Alternatively, I also know podcasters who write it all down, word for word, even for years, having done it. Slowly and surely, they would have a full script and read it out, sounding very descriptive and expert. It's all going to be fine, no points missing, and the podcast is going to go exactly as you expect.

The downside to this is that training requires a long time. You perform two tasks: writing an essay on your subject and then speaking it out. Added to that, you can always sound pretty un-spontaneous, flat, and even robotic while reading a script. It can be less entertaining and certainly less welcoming than off-the-cuff speech. You can write a bullet-pointed script, but with a decent amount of detail. Don't write it down word for word, but for every paragraph, have a prompt, so you know where you're going. You won't miss anything this way, but hopefully, you'll avoid the monotonous read-voice issue.

1.6 Environment

Even though we've talked about the quality of recording equipment, microphones, and software, the environment is one of the main variables in how your recording will sound. For good quality sound, thinking about where you make your recordings is really necessary. When deciding where to do your recording, here are a few items to think about:

On a video, background noise is even more apparent. Look out for Hallways with people passing by regularly. Close-by windows with a busy road outside. Computers or other devices in the background are working. Wide lights that create a clicking sound. Echoes can really diminish the quality of your recording: Try to record in a wide space, not facing the wall. Or try to record with wood or wallpaper in a space with soft walls. When you do your recording, here are a few things to worry about: The presenters themselves are usually the main source of unnecessary noise: paper rustling or key jangling by presenters or visitors. Coughing, sniffing, and breathing heavily.

The microphone fumbles, or the recorder moves. The primary thing is to be mindful that the microphone picks up some noise very quickly. You want to be as quiet as possible in the room you want, and you want the people in the room to be as cautious as they can't make unwanted noise.

Chapter 2: Techniques for Podcasting

When your recording is done, it's time to turn it into an edited podcast. This is where you cut out any bugs, stick various audio recordings together and add any music or sound effects. The key thing to remember here now is that you don't need to go overboard. Several effective podcasts do a very little editing. In fact, you might not need to do any editing at all if you're just trying to get your details out there. Music, FX, and multiple features are all well and well, but longevity is the key to podcasting success. The one for you is whatever process helps you to make good, daily podcasts. And if that means no music for the title and no editing, then that's all right. As long as the material is good and the audio recording quality is good, then you will do well. But there's nothing like a bit of music, some FX, and tying together a few different audio clips, such as introductions, interviews, and features, to add a bit of a professional ending. Let's see how they do it.

2.1 Edit Your Podcast

Music can make a major difference in the way that your podcast sounds professional and engaging. Your podcast will really stand out from the crowd with a brief 10-second musical intro, and that audio can be used as background music at various points to make it sound even more professional. Sound effects can also help improve your podcast, providing a little break between one audio recording and the next - for example, the introduction and an interview. There are a variety of sites on the web to find Royalty-free songs. Most of them need you to simply credit the music producer on your website or on the podcast, and you can then use the music for free as much as you want. Audacity is a very easy-to-use audio editor, but it takes a short time to work out the instruments.

Importing the audio files that you have captured is the first thing you need to do. For some fast editing, this could only be one recording, or you may be bringing together a couple of different recordings into one podcast. You can now view the imported audio file on an audio track. If you press the green play button on the top of the page, you can listen to the just imported file. You can play with this and figure out what bits you need to delete.

Cutting, Picking, and Pasting

Cutting is the simplest editing option you'll want to carry out. This means leaving out parts of the track that are unwanted. You may want to do this because, during the recording, you coughed, or you just made a mistake that you want to eliminate. Either way, you need to pick it and cut it in order to get rid of the offending bit of audio. Using the selection method to pick a section that you want to cut, copy or paste. You can quickly select it by clicking on the icon in the toolbar if it is not enabled. You will now click and drag the cursor over the section you want to pick, just as you would if you were to select a sentence in a word processor document. The region selected would appear darker than the clip's surrounding area. To pick a large part of the film, you can select a part and keep dragging it to the right. This will make Audacity scroll right for you until the end of your selection is found. I'd recommend zooming out, though, so that before beginning Playback, you can see your full range. To see the whole range, you'll have to find a balance between zooming out and zooming in enough to find the quiet point between the words or phrases that you've captured. Normally, when there is silence, the best place to cut is, and that is reflected by the wave shape falling down to nothing. To listen to the audio in the selected region, you can now click the space bar as a little trick. It helps to ensure that you've got the right part. You can press the SHIFT button to extend or contract your range and click on the position where you want the selection boundary to travel to. If you click on the spot in the center of the current selection on the right-hand side, the new selection's right-hand boundary will be set, and vice versa on the left-hand side.

Listen to the audio around the cut after you have cut out a selection to make sure it sounds OK. If you have cut in the middle of a word unintentionally, and it's really clear, then you can still undo the action and try again. In the edit menu, press Undo to do so. Instead of completely cutting out a portion of the recording, you may want to copy it elsewhere. "Copy" will copy the list to the clipboard after you've made your selection. You can then paste the selection back into any track by clicking where you want it to be put, and then in the Edit menu, selecting Paste.

Mixing a Voiceover with Background Music

It's very convenient for Audacity to blend two separate sounds together. This is known as multitrack editing, which is a step up from basic editing of audio;

if you get this far, well done then! Here are a few steps that need to be taken: Open your key audio file (for example, the interview you recorded last week). Select Audio Import... From the File menu, open the sound that you want to play next to, and (for example, the background music)—using the Play button to listen to songs. Audacity will have them put next to each other automatically, and you'll hear them playing at the same time. In the game window, you can see both tracks, one on top of the other. Choose the Time Shift method and, by dragging it left or right, change the direction of one track or another. As you have anticipated, move the tracks so they are synchronized so that the music begins and stops when you want it to. Adjust the music to fit the appropriate duration. Simply selecting a portion of it and taking it out will shorten the music. Find the point where you want it to stop, pick it right from there to the end, and click the delete key.

Acting with Music in Podcasts Volume

Music has two key purposes in a Podcast: Background music, to play alongside a voice track continuously—introduction or outro music to mark your podcast's beginning and end. You'll need to edit the volume in some way in both cases. You'll need to make it louder for background music to block out the voice stream. And you'll want to make it fade in and out for intro and outro music to fit in with the voice tracks it supports. Background music is pretty simple; you just need to reduce the whole track's volume. This is achieved on the left-hand panel of each track using the Gain control. To minimize the volume and right to raise it, slide the control left. Pressing Play, listening to the audio, and shifting the lever left and right until you hear a decent level is the best way to reach the correct level. Make sure you have soft enough background music so that the voices are very easy to hear.

Normally, for intro and outro music, you want to play the music at the beginning for a short time and then fade it out when you start talking. Using the fade method, this can be achieved very readily. Firstly, determine how long to play the intro music. Normally, 10 to 20 seconds is enough. Select the last 5 seconds or so of the music track, then. This is an area that's going to disappear. If you want a longer fade so that it overlaps with the voice for longer, then at the beginning of the track, keep a longer music segment, and pick a longer fade area. Click the Effects Menu > Fade Out tool once you have picked a region to fade out. This will start at its usual volume for the entire selected region and then gradually fade away to silence. In the following picture, you will see how this feel. The arrow displays the selected and fading region. The only thing to do now moves the voice track to match the segment of Fading, and you're done.

By overlapping the start of the voice track with the fading field, you can get the best results here. This means that as the music is fading out, the voice starts talking and provides a nice professional sounding intro. Use the time shift method to switch the voice track to the right to do this, until the beginning of it lies just beyond the beginning of the music.

The red arrow indicates where the fade begins, so I dragged the voice to the right so that it starts just after the fade starts. Try this out, and you'll be shocked at how professional you already sound! Using the Fade In the method, you can do the exact reverse for your outro music. In the Impact menu, this appears, too. Simply select the start portion of your outdoor music, press the Fade In tool, and the track will start at zero volume and gradually increase over the selected time span.

Using the Intro/Outro Music Volume Control Envelope Function

You'll want a little more power over the volume of a track sometimes. An example of this may be an intro where you've got 30 seconds of music, but you give a brief introduction to the podcast for 10 seconds in the middle of that music. This is a very popular introduction to professional podcasts, and when you can pull it off, it really makes an episode shine. Fortunately, it's pretty easy! Using the envelope method, you do this. Grab your music first and position it at the beginning of the track. Get your brief vocal introduction, then drag it to the music intro's center to overlap. You'll hardly hear the voice if you play the recording now since the music would be too noisy. Only for the segment where the voice is speaking, all you need to do is reduce the volume of the song. Pick the Envelope method to do this. You'll see that a blue line bounds the track, top, and bottom. At the point where you want the music to begin to fade down, click this blue line with the envelope method. The left-most arrow in the above image indicates this point. Next, just after the vocals start, click where you want the music to end up fading. The second red arrow from the left indicates this. You can see tiny white dots appear on the blue line when you do this, as the arrow below indicates. If you click and drag these dots up and down, you can adjust the music's volume at that point in the track.

It makes the music louder by dragging the white dots towards the middle. This is how it should look in your initial fade-out. You can see that the music starts out loud, then the music starts to will in volume just before the vocal starts (the topmost track). Then it levels out a little after the vocal begins and remains playing, but softly. For the fade back up, you simply do the reverse until the vocals end. Right before the voice begins, click on the blue line, then again just after the voice stops. Finally, drag the white dot to the top of the track right after the voice stops so that the volume increases. The track shown now looks like the picture above, and it sounds very professional! For outro music, too, this can work very well. Outro music works well when it fades early and plays during the podcast's entire closing segment. This is usually where you chat or ask for input about the next episode and send out your contact information—using your envelope method to fade out your outro music at the beginning of your closing segment to a low volume level. Then, once you are talking, fade it to full volume, play it for 5 to 10 seconds, then stop the music entirely. This gives an outro with a fine, professional tone.

2.2 Your Completed Podcast export

It's time to export the finished article after you've completed enough of your editing! Tap on file> Export to export your podcast. This will allow you to choose where the file needs to be saved. Making sure you choose the MP3 format is the important thing here. This is the most widely used podcasting style and is the one that can be processed by any digital player.

When your podcast has been registered, edited, and saved as an MP3, it is time to publish it on a Podcast Hosting site so your eager audience can listen to your efforts.

2.3 Podcast Hosting

You need a special podcast hosting space to store your podcast episodes and deliver them via an RSS feed. This helps you to upload episodes of your podcast, put alongside them a little intro text and then publish them for all to hear. The podcast hosting site will arrange the RSS feed once released and ensure that everyone can listen to your podcast if they so choose. There are a few options for hosting podcast pages, but when using The Podcast Host, I'm going to talk about the method you'll follow. The Podcast Host is based on the WordPress platform and is an easy-to-use system. WordPress is used as a foundation by many podcasting sites, so the method I will discuss next will be very similar to other podcasting sites out there. Obviously, though, it's up to you who you go with, and there are quite a few choices that you'll easily find online. You'll be asked to build an account, whatever you want, after which you'll have a site set up for you. It's time to upload a podcast to that space once your podcasting space is set up. In a similar way to blogging, podcasting works. You create a page that contains some text, and a link to your podcast usually called an article.

The text is very useful as it offers a guide to the episode of the podcast, inviting people to listen to it. Here are some pretty good things to include on a podcast episode page: Write an introduction to the podcast, providing a brief overview of the subject. Have a show time schedule, indicating when each segment begins so that the listener can easily forward through if they want to hear a specific section. Include a submission, either by comments or email, for input. To create a new episode page on the Podcast Host, select 'Podcast' on the left-hand menu, and then 'Add New.' This will create a screen. Insert the title in the uppermost box, and then the summary of the podcast episode in the larger edit box below. It is time to upload the audio file itself once you have written your message.

The method is quite clear on the Podcast Host. To find the 'Episode Info,' look underneath the Summary box. Click 'Upload File' to upload the audio file, and then you will be prompted to find your audio file. As shown below, in the center, click the Select Files button and find the file on your screen. Now, the file is going to be uploaded to the podcasting site. Enter a descriptive title and a brief description, only for your own reference, once the episode is uploaded. Tap on 'Insert to Post' then.

You can now see the Podcast Episode's specifics displayed in the 'Details of the Episode' box, such as URL, time, and height. That's what you need to do now. The audio file is attached and ready to go with the episode. Once you have reviewed everything, to finish the operation, press 'Publish.' You've got a live podcast now! By clicking the 'View Podcast' link at the top of the page, you can now view the episode page above the title. You'll see that you've automatically added a player connection so people can play your episode right from the list. They can also download it or subscribe to it on iTunes-all of the stuff we spoke about earlier in the book in the 'Listening to Podcasts' segment. All there is left to do now is let people know and get them to listen.

2.4 Being Mentioned in Your Podcast

The final step on your podcasting journey is optional, but the person who misses it out is unusual. And that's getting yourself identified in other directories and iTunes. In principle, it is now possible to find and listen to your podcast. But without being identified in the regular directories, it's unlikely anyone can find you. It's also very convenient for people to subscribe to your podcast to be included in iTunes. In the iTunes store, they will simply find you, press the subscribe button, and they're done. Listeners have to locate and manually type your Podcast feed URL into their podcatcher programmed without being listed. Let's get identified, then. I'm going to go through the process it takes to get into iTunes and then list some other resources you may want to look at.

Unsurprisingly, if you have not already done so, the first move is to download the iTunes application. You need to register your podcast from the iTunes store, and you need iTunes to access it. Load iTunes and press the button on the top right of the 'iTunes Store button.

Then, by clicking the 'Podcasts' link at the top of the page, as seen in the next screenshot, locate the iTunes store's podcast section. Here you'll see how many different podcasts are out there and the number of subjects. Yours will be one of them soon! First, look at the right-hand menu before you see 'Submit a Podcast' and scroll down. It'll be in the Fast Links Podcast section. Click 'Submit a Podcast,' and you will be prompted to enter the Podcast Feed URL. By logging into your Dashboard, clicking the Podcast connection on the left, and then clicking Settings, you will find the Feed URL on the Podcast Host. This takes you to the settings page for your podcast. Now, if you scroll to the bottom of the settings tab, a section called 'Share' will be available. You can find the Podcast Feed URL here. Copy the web address shown next to 'Full Feed' and paste it into the new Podcast Feed URL field shown in iTunes. iTunes will ask you to log in with your Apple ID if you're not already signed in. If you don't have an Apple ID, you'll have to register with Apple to get one before you can upload your podcast. After you have signed in, you can see the iTunes Podcast Information tab. This helps you to verify that all is OK with your submission. If you have already uploaded an image (found on the settings tab, the same as your feed URL) for your podcast, the image will appear. All the other information can also be edited on that tab, so if something is incorrect, just cancel it now. Then, before resubmitting your feed URL, you can go back and change the settings. Once you're satisfied, press Submit, and you're done! You will now be moderating your podcast and uploading it to the iTunes store. It might take a few days for this to go through, but they can send you an email once it is complete.

After you've launched your podcast, there are a few other services worth applying to. The stitchery is the first one I'll mention. On both iOS and Android, this is a really common app that appears. It helps people very easy to find your podcast and download and listen to it quickly. It's worth getting yourself enrolled for that purpose. Next, there are a couple of directories worth sending your information to. They are as follows: The Podcast Directory- Not called very imaginatively, but still very broad.

Podcast Alley-An institution that has been around since podcasting's early days. It's well worth saying.

Another broad directory that should get you in front of even more listeners should be Podfeed.net.

2.5 Niche Directories

Niche directories are the last thing I'll mention. To see if there are any podcast directories that specialize in your area, it is well worth taking a look around. So, if you're doing a knitting podcast, check Google to see if there is a directory for a knitting podcast or even a directory for a craft podcast. The Learn Out Loud directory, which lists only teaching Podcasts, is an example. To be honest, at some point, it is arguable that most podcasts can teach, but they have their own requirements. These specialist directories are perfect because they have much less competition, and the audience is much more focused. This ensures that you will be more likely to be spotted in the crowd and by the right kind of people. It's also possible that you're going to start getting found in the same niche by someone podcasting, and then when they mention you, you might get a little free promotion. For winning listeners, there's nothing like a bit of culture.

I hope you have been given a good introduction to the world of podcasting by this guide. I have given you enough details to create your very first podcast, and by editing and adding music, go beyond the simplest type.

Chapter 3: Availability to Your Audience

Distribution is the method that ends up in your listeners' hands with the podcast you have created and encoded. This chapter offers an overview of the distribution process, including the basics of how distribution works, RSS, podcast aggregators (sometimes referred to as podcatchers), and the various ways your media files can be hosted and distributed.

3.1 How to Work Podcast

You've created a high-quality podcast and encoded it into a high-quality encoded format suitable for distribution if you've made it this far through the novel. The next move is to get it in your audience's possession. There are three measures involved in this: 1. Creating a website where the content of your podcast is published, 2. To find and subscribe to your podcast, 3. Add your podcast to one or more of the podcasting directories so your listeners can. You must first create a website where your podcast is released by uploading your podcast episode to your website. You may want to register a domain name at this point to have a special and easy-to-find home on the web for your podcast. A blog is the easiest and most popular kind of platform for podcasters. The blog is short for "Weblog." In order to offer people a convenient way to build and update an online journal, blogging technology was created. Blogs also have RSS (Really Easy Syndication) syndication so that when you update your blog, people who want to stay in touch will subscribe to your blog and get notified. Podcasting and blogging share a history that is similar. The technology that underlies podcasts' delivery is the same technology that lets people know when you update your blog. The only distinction with podcasting is that the notification of the update contains the address to a media file, which is your podcast. The media file being inserted is known as an enclosure. Today, many blogging systems allow podcasting, adding enclosures to blog posts automatically. Make sure new listeners will find you after you build the web site to host your podcast. You have to make sure you're as easy to find as possible if you want to create an audience. When people search the web for the content they are interested in and are led to the site hosting your podcast, several podcasts are discovered. You should also make sure that your website contains plenty of information about your podcast and that it is easy for search engines to find you with your search keywords and description.

3.2 The Secret Sauce of Podcasting

The RSS file is the secret behind podcasting, actually. For Very Quick Syndication, RSS is an acronym. In the late 1990s, during the first "boom" of the Internet, companies such as Marimba, PointCast, and Data Channel offered news delivery based on a technology known as "push." When the server was ready to push the content, push technology provided information to client PCs. This proved to be technologically inefficient because the server attempted to send the data out all at once, consuming vast quantities of bandwidth and blocking private and corporate networks. A new model has emerged, called "poll then pull." In this model, before individual clients requested it, the server did not send out updated details. RSS, inspired by the different formats of content syndication used in push technology, was originally suggested in 1997 by Dave Winer while running a company called Userland. RSS was intended to allow a specific type of news syndication known as blogging today. Other companies have created versions of their own, such as RDF and CDF, such as Netscape and Microsoft. As fascinating as the RSS story is, at this point, all you really need to know is that your RSS feed is a key ingredient in your podcast's success. It's the process by which people subscribe to your new episodes and instantly receive them.

You need to follow these two steps to make it accessible to your listeners when you are ready to publish a podcast episode: Upload your media file from your computer to the server your listeners are going to download it from. They can do this either by using a podcatcher or directly from your web page. Connect your newly uploaded episode to your RSS feed so that when podcatchers review your RSS feed, they can see that it has been updated and start downloading the new podcast automatically.

By reading the RSS feed for your podcast and reviewing the results,

Podcatchers "check your feed" daily. It downloads it if the podcatcher sees an episode that is dated later than the last episode it downloaded. Some services/blogging services for media distribution update the RSS automatically. It is very simple as adding a new episode to your RSS feed if you want to do it manually. Adding a new episode to an RSS feed involves using XML tags to add information to the current feed. This sounds trickier than it really is. While some users come to your website, click the link to an individual podcast, and listen to a particular episode, most podcast listeners use an aggregator called a dedicated program that reviews your RSS feed regularly and downloads new episodes as you publish them. Aggregators that are programmed exclusively for podcast subscriptions are often referred to as podcatchers. Even if you do not want to place your podcast content on a portable music system, we suggest using a podcatcher because it allows the automated downloading process and offers a convenient way to browse your ever-growing content collection. You have to place your podcast files on a server that can be accessed through HTTP for people to be able to download your podcast (hypertext transfer protocol). Since HTTP is the protocol used to distribute web pages, whether you already have a website or a website host, you can put your podcasts on your web server. Alternatively, it inevitably requires access to a server where you can put your podcasts if you've signed up for a podcast hosting account. You should be aware of the storage and bandwidth problems surrounding podcasting, whether you are hosting your own server, using a website hosting service, or a podcast hosting service. You may be familiar with web hosting accounts where a certain amount of storage and throughput for your website is allocated to you. Be cautious if you want to host your podcast on your website, as podcast files are considerably larger than web pages and images. Podcast files, therefore, have a huge effect on your storage and throughput. You may wish to consider working with one of the various services that can host your podcast files at some point. With plenty of different service packages and pricing systems, there are plenty of them. Do plenty of homework and select a host for a podcast that provides the best support for you.

A technology called RSS is at the center of podcasting delivery (Really Simple Syndication). More and more blogging solutions and hosting services for podcasts provide automated solutions to take care of your RSS feed, so you don't have to think about it. But it's helpful to learn the nuts and bolts of RSS and know-how podcasting works. Initially, RSS was designed to allow news and other textual information to be transmitted automatically. RSS established a system where consumer applications could decide if new content on news websites was available. These programmers, commonly referred to as aggregators, showed the news headlines and made it easier for individuals to track news from a range of different outlets. It was not that long before people found out that it was possible to use the RSS standard to fuel a distribution revolution.

RSS has been around in several different formats for years. The RSS culture was catalyzed by the blogging boom when individuals requested a way to track a vast number of their favorite bloggers. RSS features have started to be integrated into applications for blogging. What made podcasting possible were the enclosures. People had already subscribed to blogs from each other, and a lot of bloggers were playing with audio. It instantly became as simple to add audio to an existing feed as to add a line of code to the existing RSS feed. An audio experiment turned into a content explosion within a year. In its simplicity lies the elegance of the RSS. An RSS feed includes data about your podcast and about your podcast's individual episodes. You add details to your feed about the new episode each time you make a new episode of your podcast. On your side of the equation, that is what you have to think about.

Your listeners are on the other side. A podcast aggregator, such as iTunes or FireAnt, would be used by them. What they actually do when they listen to your podcast is told their podcast programmed to regularly review your RSS feed to see if anything has been added. The app lets the listener know that a new episode is available if and when anything is inserted and automatically installs the episode (if that is how they have their software configured). It's essentially that. We'll split the method into six separate steps to add a little more detail:

1. You make a media file for your podcast and upload it to a server. Sometimes, this is the same server that hosts your blog and RSS feed; sometimes, on separate servers, they are hosted.

2. You're changing your RSS feed to show that a new episode of your podcast has been uploaded. In one of two ways, you can do this:

a. Using Web-based blogging tools or using a program that speaks to your blogging software, you write a blog entry, often containing display notes, and post it to your website. You state that there is an associated file when you post your blog entry and enter the link in the tag.

b. Using either a text editor or a tool (such as FeedForAll, Feeder, Podifer, WebPod), you manually build your RSS feed and upload the modified RSS file to your Web server.

3. Either by clicking your RSS link or inserting the URL for your feed into a podcast aggregator like iTunes, Juice, or Doppler, listeners who are interested in your podcast subscriptions.

4. In order to see that if anything new has been added, the podcast aggregator regularly checks your RSS feed.

5. The media files are downloaded using the URL defined in the tags when

the podcast aggregator detects new things with enclosures.

6. The podcasts are transferred directly to a portable media player after the download has ended (if that is what the listener has specified).

Basically, what you have to do is update your RSS feed, and remember to upload your site with the modified feed. The remainder arises automatically. But how do you get your RSS feed updated? For the most part, you'll probably be using a basic tool, but you should know what is inside the RSS feed and why before we show you the tools.

An RSS feed is simply a text file that contains your podcast content. An Extensible Markup Language (XML), RSS feeds are written, indicating that all the information is stored inside or surrounded by tags. You won't be too scared by an RSS feed if you have ever looked at HTML code, the language used to build Web pages. The official RSS default defines a single XML document that describes a channel that contains one or more objects, each of which contains individual blocks of content. Content blocks contain the actual details found in the feed, such as the title and content summary. For podcasting, the items contain at least a connection to a media file that uses an optional element called an enclosure and usually contained a summary element that defines the media. Actually, RSS feeds are very simple. In reality, looking at one is the easiest way to learn about them. You can see that they're just a highly organized way of arranging knowledge if you can get through all the angle brackets. Let's look at a straightforward RSS feed and then describe each of the elements.

Apple has developed a variety of tags attached to an RSS feed to get more detail about podcasts available in the iTunes store. To get featured placement on the iTunes podcast page, they are required. Of course, there is no guarantee that you will earn a featured spot, but it is a good idea not to disqualify your podcast from consideration by leaving them out.

Using a text or XML editor is the simplest, but not the fastest, way to construct an RSS feed. You need to pay close attention to detail, be familiar with XML syntax, and have your podcast media files' full descriptions to use this approach. In particular, you need to know your media file's URL, size, and MIME type. Lots of text editors are available. Make sure you're using a simple text editor if you're going this road, not a program like WordPad or Microsoft Word. Although these are excellent word processing applications, they're not ideal for creating XML files. The explanation is that not everything they placed in a file is revealed to you by word processors. They actually have a lot of information about formatting that is hidden from you. This knowledge about formatting, however, is not true in an XML file. There are some examples of text editors you can use: n Notepad (Windows), n BBEdit (Mac), n VI (Linux). It's pretty easy to edit in a simple text editor. You do not have any special tools; you are just typing in raw XML. One thing you can do is to download from another podcast an existing RSS feed and replace the text with text relevant to your podcast. Be careful not to leave text from the feed you're copying while you're doing this.

Another thing to note is that the tag's length and form parameters must include file size and MIME types. For these, you must use the right values, or your RSS feed is not going to work. The size of your file in bytes is the length parameter. Depending on your operating system, you can get this by clicking on the file's properties in Finder or Explorer.

General-purpose XML editors offer you more features, including automatic reformatting, syntax checking, and highlighting, than simple text editors. It is easy to reformat because it makes your RSS feeds easier to read automatically. Testing the syntax guarantees that the file is actually a legitimate XML file. The highlighting function allows the "light up" valid XML tags in a particular color. This is a fantastic feature because you get a visual hint if you erroneously type a tag wrongly because it stays in black and white.

3.3 Dedicated Authoring Tools for RSS Feeds

If your podcast hosting solution does not have any form of automated RSS feed creation tool, a dedicated RSS tool is probably better used. These tools are designed to do one thing well—RSS feeds from the author. They're crude sometimes and don't give a lot of functionality, but they're certainly going to generate legitimate RSS feeds, which is what you're after. FeedForAll is a tool available for both Windows and Macintosh to build RSS feeds. It's a fill-in-the-blanks form-based tool that makes RSS construction quick. Actually, it couldn't be simpler to use the wizard to build your RSS feed. FeedForAll is offered as a trial for 30 days, after which you have to buy a license. There are three tabs on the FeedForAll interface that allow you to edit information about feeds, objects, and images. The Feeds tab provides a list of RSS feeds and allows both the necessary and optional data to be entered as part of the RSS tag. Creating, copying, uploading, and previewing features are also available from the toolbar's menus and icons. It asks if you want to use the wizard to build your RSS feed the first time you run FeedForAll. FeedForAll has a basic guy for novices based on a wizard.

Regardless of how you build your RSS feed, you can make your life a little easier with other useful RSS tools. To ensure that your RSS file uses the right syntax, feed validators are used. Feedburner still provides confirmation but adds your feed's statistical monitoring so that you can track how well your podcast is performing. Feed validators evaluate your RSS file's contents and inform you whether the syntax is valid or not. These tools are useful, especially if you manually build your RSS feed. Even if you are using an XML editor, feed validators are helpful since, in addition to checking the XML syntax, they also check to ensure that your media file exists at the URL you specified in your feed. Every podcaster would like to know how many people listen to their podcast. The majority of podcast hosting services provide reasonably easy access to the data. However, you can use Feedburner to get statistics about your audience if you're hosting your own website and podcast, or if your host does not have statistics. You build your RSS feed and then insert the URL for your feed into a Feedburner page when you use Feedburner. Feedburner analyses and lets you know if there is something wrong with your RSS feed. The custom URL you want for your RSS file can be specified. This redirects the RSS traffic through the Feedburner servers so that both statistics and an optional monetization opportunity based on ads can be generated. Feedburner also provides a service called SmartCast that reads your current RSS feed and automatically generates a new RSS feed, based on links to MP3 files in your blog posts, containing enclosure tags. This is especially helpful for those who use blogging systems such as Blogger and MSN Spaces that don't have native podcasting support.

Feedburner also has a variety of other features that podcasters may be interested in. For instance, it provides a "widget" that you can add to your blog that provides a real-time overview of your podcast listeners' number. You may not want to do this when you start off, but it can look pretty impressive if you have thousands of registered subscribers. Using Feedburner has one possible drawback. Routing all of your RSS traffic via Feedburner gives a certain amount of control over your feed to Feedburner. Anyone using the Feedburner URL who subscribes to your podcast will expect to find your podcast there. If you ever plan to avoid using Feedburner, it can be hard to move individuals to your new RSS feed.

What makes listening to a podcast possible is SS feeds. N RSS feeds quick XML files that include your podcast details and a real media file link. N RSS can be manually generated in plain text or XML editors. N Dedicated applications for RSS authoring provide better features than text editors, and to make sure it works; it's important to "validate" your RSS feed.

3.4 Your Podcast Finds A Home

It's time to figure out how the RSS feed fits into your website, where to put it so that people can find it, and how to keep it updated, now that you have an understanding of what RSS is and how to create an RSS file. It's not that hard, but there are a variety of different ways to do it, so you should think about how you want your podcast and your website to be handled in the long term. You have to make a range of choices that reflect on your podcast's two main aspects, your website, and your media. The decision you make now have a direct impact on your supply chain and influence your long-term planning as well. It can be hard to change your strategy mid-stream after you launch your podcast and crank up your web site. We hope that you will have a clearer understanding of the problems and how you're going to deal with them after reading this part. Let's start with an overview of the various ways that you can market your website and podcast, along with some of each option's basic advantages and disadvantages.

All we've really addressed so far is how to create your podcast media file, and we've talked a bit about creating your RSS feed. There's another aspect of your performance that can be just as critical: your website. Podcasting started as a way for blogs to add audio and to have this audio transferred to an iPod automatically. Since then, however, the notion of podcasting has evolved. Informal studies have shown that up to 50 percent of all podcasts are watched when seated in front of a computer. Many of these can be played in iTunes' background, but a large number are still watched as embedded presentations on web pages. The purists in podcasting are quick to suggest that these aren't really podcasts. (Some simply claim that something other than an MP3 file is not a podcast.) Call it what you want: Using RSS feeds, a lot of programming is generated and distributed on the Internet. It is possible to encounter this programming in several distinct ways. The question is, what kind of experience do you want to have with your audience? We can divide the various choices into three key categories of ways to host your podcast in an attempt to enforce some form of order on this chaos: on a website or blog you run and maintain yourself, on a controlled website or blogging service, on a dedicated podcast hosting service Each of these has advantages and disadvantages. In a nutshell, you'll have the most versatility and independence if you're prepared to take on the responsibility of managing and maintaining your platform. This versatility comes at a price, however. You just have to think about lots of things if you're operating your own platforms, such as software upgrades, hackers, spammers, and hardware issues. You have much less to think about if you use regulated or dedicated systems, but this ease of use comes at the expense of versatility. You might not be able to install some new gadget on your website that you discovered on an open-source platform, or because of support problems, you may not be able to integrate the latest video technology. In a little more depth, let's talk about the options.

3.5 Managing A Website of Your Own

It can be lots of fun maintaining your own website, but it can also be a lot of work. First, you have to either create a server or purchase space from a Web hosting service on a shared server. Some providers of web hosting provide unlimited access to the operating system so that you can tinker with the desire of your heart, while others impose fairly serious limits on what you can and cannot do. The good thing about hosting your own site, when you like, is the utter freedom to do what you want. You can add forums, install a wiki (a public space where people can add and edit content at will), change the look of your home page, or do something else that catches your fancy, assuming you are running on your own server and have complete access to the operating system. You don't have to wait before a host introduces new characteristics; you just add them yourself. This implies, of course, that you are very comfortable operating a server and downloading software. These days, several blog and content management system (CMS) software packages are built relatively painlessly. However, if anything breaks down at the end of the day, you don't have anybody to call. All is just fine until something breaks, at which point it can become a nightmare to run your own server, particularly if your podcast gets popular and your audience is baying for more. Another concern is scalability. The traffic to your website will spike if your podcast becomes wildly popular or if iTunes chooses to put you on the home page of the podcast directory for some reason. Web servers are not that difficult, but they can break down, and if they do, the most inconvenient time for them to do so is almost always due to a massive increase in traffic. "If your podcast is so popular that you fry the small server at the end of your home DSL line, chances are good that you will be able to afford a new server or afford to move to a managed hosting service, as the saying goes in the world of start-ups, having capacity problems is "a good problem to have.

Only if you're a seasoned Internet veteran with access to some decent server hardware and some spare time should you attempt to run your own server? A managed hosting service or a dedicated podcasting hosting service should be considered if you're just starting out.

Using A Controlled Provider for Hosting

Using a controlled hosting service is the next step forward in the hosting world. There are hundreds of different hosting solutions out there, literally. The chances are that the company you use to register your URL can provide some kind of hosting service for your site when you register the URL for your podcast. Every month, hosting packages normally provide a certain amount of free storage and throughput, and when you surpass any of these, you incur overage charges. Some hosting services come with pre-packaged software that allows you to build pre-existing templates for a website or a content management system that allows you to manage your website easily. You'll need e-commerce features if you're thinking about having e-commerce on your web. Many hosting service providers have features for a "shopping cart" and may even be able to process credit card transactions for you. Statistics about the website traffic are one thing you'll want to make sure that the service provides. You will need reliable traffic statistics to gauge your programming's popularity and attract potential sponsors and advertisers if you are serious about turning your podcast into a company. As much statistical knowledge as you can find, you can look for it. A variety of uniform bundles of Web stats are satisfactory, but the best hosting companies would offer extremely comprehensive stats. Perhaps the best thing about using a controlled hosting service is that you take off your plate a huge amount of responsibility. You no longer have to think about hardware, and the hosting partner's concern is that of spammers and hackers. You should also be able to foresee when you're going to run out of space and collaborate with the hosting partner to add more capacity if the statistics indicate a strong upward trend. The only downside to using a managed hosting service is that the software that you may install can be restricted. It depends on the type of service that you buy. You can buy a shared server; in which case you are typically very limited since not only you but the other clients on the same server need to be a stable hosting environment for the server. Hundreds of other Web pages could be running off the same shared server. In general, hosting services also provide dedicated servers, where you simply rent hardware from them, and they keep it up and running. Similar hosting providers permit different access levels. Some encourage you to do whatever you want to do, while others restrict what you can do so that the computer meets the quality, making it easier for them to maintain. The service you choose largely depends on how much flexibility you want to install software and change it.

Controlled hosting services that are highly tailored for the needs of a podcaster are dedicated podcast hosting services. These platforms, for instance, typically provide tools to build and update your RSS feed. Some form of a wizard can also automate them, so your RSS feed is automatically modified when you upload a new media file. Many dedicated podcast hosting services often provide their customers with some kind of website, usually in the form of a blog. Often, blogs come with their own URL, so you can have a very personalized Web address.

Some podcasting hosting services have themselves become hubs, either because they host other common podcasts or because they have been around long enough that people know that it is a good place to find podcasts. Another persuasive argument to go with a dedicated podcast hosting service might be this. They already have an audience looking for podcasts, and there's a fair chance that if you're the young kid on the block, they'll check out your podcast. You probably won't have a lot of flexibility to change these services on your website because they are so highly specialized to start with. You do not own all the real estate on your Web page, either. For example, in order to recover some of its costs, the hosting service can reserve the right to advertise on your Web page. They may want to place an ad on your podcast as well. It's not shocking that they want to try to make a bit of money from your podcast, seeing as all of these podcast hosting services offer away a serious number of resources and storage. The territory comes with it.

It's really just an option to run and host your own website if you are very savvy or if you already have an entire framework to which you add a podcast. You can run into problems with scaling, but you'll be able to solve them because of your savvy, right? If you're experienced, using a controlled web hosting solution is a great choice for your website. The more Web-savvy you are, the more a managed solution you can get out of. You're going to have a URL of your own and the right to do what you want on your web. If you're just starting out and don't know anything about websites, using a dedicated podcast hosting service is a brilliant idea. You can't beat the ease, and they let you concentrate on programming, which is what you need to do anyway. If you stop growing the service, when you get to it, you can cross the bridge. One thing to mention is that this doesn't need to be a case of either/or. For e.g., with a managed hosting solution, you might host your website and then use the dedicated podcast hosting service only to host the podcast file! Just because you have a simple web site provided by a podcast hosting solution does not mean you have to use it. In fact, for the savvier consumer, this is probably the best choice. To host your podcast media files, use a hosting podcasting service, and you'll be able to take advantage of its RSS software, its statistics, and any other special tools it can offer. Then, with a Web hosting service, host your domain, complete with your customized URL, so you can have more flexibility with your site.

3.6 Your Domain Registration

Registering a domain for your site is important because that's your address on the server. Sure, you can get a sub-domain on another site, which is fine for amateurs, but if you're serious, you just want a URL of your own. It's easy to register a domain after you find a URL you want that hasn't already been registered. The last part is key: while the number of letter combinations that make up a URL is almost infinite; the number of good URLs is definitely not. This is why so many Internet start-ups have such curious names; anything that hasn't been registered yet has to be invented! If a URL is open, any registrar will tell you. Simply type the URL in the form and check if it is already registered. There are lots of registrars out there, and everyone is going to do that. Only break out the credit card and record it after you find a URL that has not been registered. The cost depends on how many years you have to register for it. You can then set up a website and e-mail accounts after your domain has been registered. As a part of a package deal, your registrar can give these. These days, the Web hosting market is highly competitive. Beware, however, because the margins are getting so small that having thousands and thousands of customers is the only way these businesses can possibly make money. To see how they react to customer concerns, be sure to check out your future host's forums. To see who is getting the highest ratings for service and reliability, search rating pages. Many hosts often make it possible for you to "test drive" their service to see what their instruments can do. It is just like buying a car to find a successful Web host; take a bunch out for a spin and buy the best one you can afford with the features you need.

It is important to find out what features to look for in a hosting service, and to do so; you have to determine what kind of website you want. Many podcasts, because of their shared history, are related to a blog. For distribution purposes, they're both episodic and use RSS. And some blogs have built-in support for podcasting. However, there's no excuse because your website needs to be confined to a blog. Blogs are not inherently restrictive, but they are designed for a particular reason. There's a simple guy who allows the site owner to post regularly and post comments to readers. Blogs take care of archiving old posts automatically, and to further organize the posts; you can use tags or categories. Blogs also allow you to create static pages, such as a page that discusses the author and the podcast. All in all, they are a pretty perfect podcast den. You may want even more features on your site, however. You may want a wiki, for example, where you can identify words that are used in your podcast, and your audience may contribute. You may want to have a forum to address issues related to a specific podcast episode but not necessarily included in it. Slide shows, Flash animations, a shop selling t-shirts, and mugs, or any number of other devices available on the web could be included. You may want to have a more conventional website in this situation, with the podcast and the blog as a part of the site, maybe. Blogs do not generally remove all of this functionality, but the program is definitely not built in. And since blog software is built to do one thing well, it may not be easy to incorporate these extra functionalities. It sure isn't difficult, but it takes a little bit of know-how. So, before you first leap in feet and install some apps, it's a good idea to think about what you need from your website right now and what you're going to need within six months or a year. Preplanning will save you a lot of pain later on. When you make the decision on where to host your podcast and what programmed you will use, ownership is another thing to bear in mind. Another way of thinking about this is to use the brand definition. Your podcast, website, URL, and everything related to your output are part of your brand if you spend a lot of time and effort on making a good podcast. Building a popular podcast goes hand in hand with a successful brand being created. Effective businesses have what's called brand value. That is why companies that produce soft drinks are highly protective of their names. They know their brands' inherent worth, and they don't want someone else to benefit from them. As you build your podcasting empire, you should be thinking the same way. You want the rewards from that performance to come back to you, not your podcast hosting partner or your web hosting partner if your podcast becomes wildly popular. These individuals may play an important part in your success, but they're only hosting businesses without your success. You're the one at the table bringing the programming. It's critical that you seriously consider keeping ownership of anything relevant to your podcast for this purpose. We discussed earlier in this chapter that you should register your podcast URL, which is a prime reason. You're surrendering some of your brand value if you're hosting your site on someone else's service. You're also building someone else's brand as your brand builds, so everyone coming to your site sees your hosting partner's branding. This is not actually a bad thing; in fact, you could create your brand on the strength of an established podcast directory brand. However, in the long run, you want to be able to concentrate on making your own brand, not anyone else's.

A better solution is to retain control of your RSS feed so that all your subscribers come in and subscribe through your RSS feed via your website. So, you can change hosts, websites, or podcasts at will, and your audience won't notice anything. If you change web hosting partners, through the magic of the Internet's Domain Name System, people can always find your website (DNS). They just type mypikepodcast.com, and your website pops up, presto. Similarly, you just have to change your enclosure tags' contents in your RSS feed if you are changing hosts for your media files, and no one will ever notice. Granted, it might not be for everybody to run their own web site and maintain their own RSS feeds. A significant amount of responsibility and technical know-how is needed. There is a reason why podcast hosting companies are popular: It is difficult to pass up the convenience. If you decide to go the hosted path, just note that if your podcast is as good as you hope it would be, you will be faced with a hard decision later.

The chances are high that if you're careful about listing your podcast, you'll get most of your listeners from the larger directory services. That's not the only way of getting subscribers, though. Quite a few, particularly if your subject is unique, can find your Web page through a search engine. It is necessary to showcase your podcast on your web page in this case. In a split second, you want tourists to know that your Web page is more than just a blog. You want them to see that you have a podcast and that a single, easy-to-find button enables them to subscribe. Until recently, the problem was that no single widely recognized icon existed to signify that a podcast was available. Various icons and various colors were used for different pages. Some people took the original RSS symbol, which was a small orange box with the "RSS" letters in white and replaced the "POD" letters. The good people at the Mozilla Foundation agreed that it would be best if a generic icon were created. The reasoning behind the production was that no abbreviations or acronyms should be used in the symbol because people would not actually know what XML or RSS stood for, nor should they have to.

For hosting your podcast, there are three simple options: hosting it on your own website, hosting it on a controlled web hosting service, or using a dedicated podcast hosting service. Dedicated podcast hosting services are a perfect way to get started for an aspiring podcaster. It is a good idea to use a controlled web host since it helps you to have your own domain and URL. It is only for the seasoned, tech-savvy few to operate their own web servers. Register your podcast domain, even if you're not using it at first. Try to maintain as much control of your name as possible. This includes your URL, your URL for your RSS feed, and everything else that your podcast relates to. There is a variety of great podcast hosting services available. To advertise your feed, be sure to use the right RSS icons. If you provide your podcast media file with a direct connection, be sure to use a metafile. Consider using your site's embedded player to let people play your podcast without having to download or subscribe to it.

Chapter 4: Distributing Your Media File

One of the amazing things about podcasting is that, like streaming media, it doesn't need any special server tools. All you have to do is put the file on your Web server and update your RSS feed, and you are done. When you start out and have a handful of loyal subscribers, that is all well and healthy. But when your podcast becomes enormously successful, what happens? Different incidents happen. Next, you're unexpectedly sending out thousands of copies of your MP3 files instead of uploading a handful of MP3 files to your listeners. You're looking at a 5 MB file if your podcast is 5 minutes long and encoded at 128 Kbps. A thousand downloads mean 5 GB of throughput is what you're talking about.

You're talking around over 150 GB per month if you have a regular broadcast. That's a pretty serious traffic rate. Things are changing dramatically on this scale. Your Web server is now running all day long instead of sending out a few files when your friends search to see if you've updated your blog. That means spinning the disc drives and putting a lot of wear and tear on the machines.

For this reason, servers have a far shorter shelf life than desktop computers. Many hosting companies schedule servers that last about three years until they need to be replaced. This means, of course, that your podcast will become popular enough to attract a wide audience. Maybe that isn't the situation. Niche content that is devotedly followed by a loyal few might be your podcast. Your options for storing your media files break down as follows, regardless of your audience's size for the time being: n Host it on your web server. N Host it on a network for content delivery (CDN). N Host it on a hosting podcast site. Using peer-to-peer allocation. n We speak about each of these possibilities in a little more detail in the following pages.

4.1 Using Your Web Server

Hosting your podcast media files right on your Web server is the easiest scenario. This is probably the way to go when you're starting out. These days, most web hosting contracts generally provide a decent amount of bandwidth, which covers a fair number of downloads. Through placing hundreds if not thousands of websites on each server, the only way they can deliver these kinds of prices is. With lots of other people, you will be sharing money. This might not be a concern in some situations. However, it can be troublesome often. Your listeners might have to wait longer to download your pages and your podcast files. With the amount of storage and throughput they offer away, prices like this are pretty hard to pass up when you first start off. Many of these services also have fairly comprehensive toolsets that allow you to create e-commerce pages, blogs, and forums for web sites, and they will even host your e-mail. It's very important to merge the comparison sites and your potential partners' forums if you're thinking of going this way. See what people are thinking about them and whether they are satisfied with their current customers. Don't just go through the testimonials they put on their home page; if you can, dig into their message boards and hunt to death for them. It's not that the few dollars a month would ruin your budget; it's more that it can be a frustrating process to adjust once you're settled into a web host. The ratings for Web hosting services are updated frequently by a variety of sites out there. Only look for "best web hosting," and you're going to have a range to choose from.

4.2 Use a Hosting Service Podcast

Podcast hosting services are somewhat similar to Web hosting services but with podcaster-facing product offerings. You normally get a certain amount of storage space and throughput, and you can get a website or blog, tools to build your RSS feed, and statistics about your podcast, depending on the service. For those who are not technically savvy, the resources that podcast hosting services provide make them a great bet. In addition, many of the podcast hosting services use an unusual model where they charge for the amount of storage that you use but do not charge for output. If your podcast becomes incredibly successful, this is a fascinating approach and a great deal. However, using a podcast hosting service as described in the previous chapter means giving up some of your ownership, so you won't be able to use your own site URL. However, you can use a hybrid approach where you host your website on a web host and a podcast hosting service for your media file. You will still have access to the RSS tools, and you could either host your website's RSS feed or point to the podcast hosting service's RSS feed. It's a little awkward in that instead of the one, you're using two different programmers, but you may be able to get the best of both worlds this way. Another advantage of some hosting services is that they can provide the ability to help pay for your podcast through ads or sponsorship.

4.3 Use A Network for Content Delivery

Content Delivery Networks (CDNs) are designed to rapidly and reliably distribute large amounts of traffic. Although there may be hundreds of servers in a single location on a web host, a CDN has several data centers, and the data is normally distributed in each data center. This is done both for data integrity, so that your files are still accessible if there is a power outage anywhere and for speed. In order to make downloads happen quicker, most CDNs often depend on caching. Caching is a system where the most common files are cached at different locations so that the request does not have to go all the way back to the origin server when they are requested. Let's say CNN.com, for instance, has an incredibly famous story on its home page. The servers of origin are most likely located in Atlanta, where CNN is based. A copy and all the pictures are sent from Atlanta to Los Angeles when anyone in Los Angeles requests the CNN home page for the first time. A copy is then placed in a cache somewhere on the west coast so that it can be served directly from the local cache and not re-requested from the origin server in Atlanta the next time anyone requests that page. CDNs have premium distribution facilities, so you won't find pricing as you would with the Web hosting services. CDNs also tend to deal in very big amounts, so you shouldn't waste your time calling CDNs if you're not planning to spend hundreds of dollars a month. However, a CDN is your best bet when your podcast is at a point where you have a wide audience that demands quality service. The CDN market is mostly divided into "tier 1" suppliers with the largest and quickest networks and "tier 2" suppliers with slightly more aggressive pricing but may not provide the same service. In terms of their availability, CDNs are also classified, which some brag about in terms of 'five nines.' This means that 99.999 percent of the time, their network is available. The response time, which is the average amount of time it takes for a CDN to answer a request, is another metric used to grade CDNs—a number of services rates CDNs according to their results from time to time. In the last few years, the CDN industry has seen a lot of consolidation, and prices have fallen considerably. In order to stay competitive, the efficiency of the tier 2 CDNs has come so close to the tier 1 providers that the tier 1 providers have had to lower their rates. Some also doubt whether there is an adequate distinction between providers to further classify them into distinct levels.

4.4 Using Sharing from Peer-To-Peer

The last sharing process that you might want to consider is peer-to-peer. Instead of sending it from a single centralized server, peer-to-peer (P2P), sharing utilizes other individuals on the network to distribute files. With the arrival of Napster, which was initially used to transfer music files over the Internet, P2P sharing came to prominence. It has gone mainstream since then, with several different forms of data being transmitted in this fashion. Currently, Skype, the start-up for Internet telephony, is a P2P programmed. There are a variety of different P2P methods, but essentially the way it works is that if you request a file and the P2P network knows that someone near you already has a copy of the file, instead of sending another copy all the way through the network, you are guided to the machine of that person to get a copy. Downloads are often spread through many devices, so you're downloading parts of a file on the P2P network from several different users. P2P distribution benefits from exploiting the bandwidth of the audience, so you don't have to pay for the production. Instead, users on the network are guided to other entities, and they're using their bandwidth, not yours. P2P distribution, however, really only works if your content is quite popular.

We'll look at BitTorrent in order to explore how peer-to-peer distribution works. BitTorrent is the best-known P2P scheme, perhaps. By some estimates, there is a significant amount of BitTorrent traffic on the Internet, up to 35 percent of the traffic at any given time. It's anybody's guess what all this traffic is and whether it's legal or not. Nonetheless, it's an established structure that works well. A protocol that specifies how files can be exchanged between two or more hosts is BitTorrent. It is also the name of one of the applications that use the BitTorrent protocol to share files. Essentially, by splitting large files into several small bits, BitTorrent operates. Downloads from BitTorrent are not performed sequentially, like normal downloads from FTP or HTTP. Instead, files are downloaded by BitTorrent clients in bits, from as many different clients as possible. By checking in with a BitTorrent tracker, which keeps track of anyone who participates in sharing a specific file, BitTorrent clients find out about the various locations from which they can download files. It might seem a little complicated, but it's pretty easy, actually. Here is an instance of how it works:

1. For the file you want to distribute, you create a "torrent." This is a tiny file containing all the details that individuals need to know about the file to download it. Your BitTorrent programmed will generate a torrent.

2. It is put on a Web server after the torrent is developed and registered with what is known as a tracker. The tracker keeps track of anyone who is interested in the file distribution.

3. Next, the file has to be seeded. This means getting the distribution of the original copy of the file. This is usually achieved from the desktop of the user. On the Web site, you click the torrent connection and indicate on your BitTorrent client that you are seeding this file.

4. When the first member of the audience clicks on the torrent connection, their BitTorrent client opens the torrent file. The BitTorrent client figures out who is interested in the distribution via the tracker. The BitTorrent client starts downloading the file from the original seed file, which is your device in this situation since nobody else is.

5. He learns that there are now two devices involved in the distribution when the next user clicks the torrent connection and then checks in with the tracker: the original and the crowd's first member. Their BitTorrent client asks all clients for parts of the file.

6. The distribution becomes more and more distributed as more clients enter

the torrent, enabling clients to download the file from several different clients. Many people participating in the torrent have files that are very common, so the distribution process scales accordingly.

7. The "etiquette" of BitTorrent dictates that once you have downloaded the file, it is good to keep your BitTorrent client on for a while so that you can help spread the file to other users. This is a simplistic picture of how P2P distribution works, but it's right, basically. It needs a lot of customers to participate in the distribution to be successful for P2P distribution. So, P2P sharing gives very little value when you're first starting out because your audience will most likely download at various times and won't be able to take advantage of the distributed download. Then you might make a case for P2P delivery if your podcast audience is in the thousands.

We have easily missed up to this point because any podcatching programmed does not implement P2P software. Podcatchers may use HTTP to download MP3 files but are unable to engage in a P2P sharing scheme. So, your audience must download and install P2P distribution software if you want to use P2P as a distribution scheme. Given the antipathy that certain people have to install apps, this might not be the simplest sale. P2P sharing is commonly used for the distribution of new updates and bug fixes by the gaming community. It's a proven delivery technology that can save you a lot of money at the expense of bandwidth. However, the issue is that it is not yet incorporated in any significant way into podcasting. While P2P could be an efficient way to scale podcasting distribution in the near future, you are probably better off sticking to other distribution methods for the time being.

Many web hosting companies have insane storage and bandwidth deals but note that plenty of other users can share the service with you. This can lead to more loading times and waits. N Podcast hosting services usually have unrestricted throughput and charge for the amount of storage you use. Podcast hosting services typically come with plenty of tools that make them a great option for the less technically experienced podcaster or for people just starting out. Premium distribution services are provided through content delivery networks (CDNs) but at a premium price. The Peer-to-Peer (P2P) sharing allows files to be distributed from a range of different sources rather than from a single centralized server. P2P distribution may be an efficient way of scaling podcasting distribution in the future, but it is probably best to use other distribution methods before it is incorporated into current podcasting applications.

Chapter 5: The Business of Podcasting

Making a podcasting company may follow many distinct routes, from offering services to actually designing and producing shows and even acting as the on-air talent. This is the simple primer on the costs of podcasting-real costs are involved, and how you can prepare the company's growth, you plan to begin. Like any company, if you are very well-financed, podcasting must start smoothly. It takes a while, maybe a long time, to hit break-even if you want to make very big money because, through marketing campaigns, you have to expand your audience as well as pay to produce and distribute your audio or video programming. If your goal is to start and remain small, you should also understand how you can reduce your expenses so that your bank account or your time is not drained by the podcast away from what the bills paid. Growing a big hit, a show with tens or hundreds of thousands of listeners, means preparing for bandwidth, storage costs, publicity, and the increasing production expense that comes with the demands of high-quality programming from listeners and advertisers. You're going to start tiny, but your podcast can become the platform for stardom with the right mix of knowledge and personality.

5.1 Comprehension of Expenses Before Gains

If you started a flower shop, you'd know that at the retail location you chose, as well as for your time or that of staff, the company will have to operate on a tight budget for rent, utilities, decor, and equipment. You'll also have publicity and advertisement expenses. Have we discussed insurance? Accountancy? These same facts, considering the numerous physical and delivery variables in podcasting, are key to laying the groundwork for success when we begin to imagine a podcasting company. You'll learn a tough lesson if you believe the hype that podcasting costs little to nothing. As your show gains popularity or simply as your archives expand, even the "cheap" hosting offers advertised to podcasters come with growing costs. With slower downloads and occasional service interruptions, small audiences and advertisers can survive, but as you expand and, particularly, as you charge advertisers or subscribers for your programming, quality of service problems can drive your hosting and delivery costs higher.

Similarly, you need to make as much of your catalog available as possible to take advantage of the digital delivery climate; a person demonstrates that the doorways to broader subscriber relationships are the appeal to narrowly oriented audience desires. You virtually need to preserve the archives with the "long tail" approach to marketing. The idea that you can save money by taking offline older podcasts can sound rational, but before its full meaning has been realized, it is like discarding all your hard work. You have the chance to harvest value from older productions practically forever in the "long-tail" marketplace, and those shows were too hard to work to throw them away! You can be assured that anything you documented two years ago will be of interest to some individuals who will become loyal listeners today by sampling those old programmers.

It is important to justify any expense. You may feel good about an extraordinary microphone that costs $1,400, but is it worth the money? "Audiophiles are going to argue, "Yeah! But the difference can never be heard by the viewer. Equipment costs should be held to a minimum, especially early on, so that you have more money and resources to bring the show into development (that is, the time you don't have to work at anything else to pay for your podcasting habit). Similarly, having all your old shows on the Net is a fantastic way to get your work discovered by new listeners, but if you're considering putting up shows that are unrelated to what you do today, your old cooking audio might not get you any new followers if you are podcasting about sports today, you might want to think twice about the cost. Spend money on cost-justified smart ideas, which will ultimately deliver a return greater than the money that you sink into them. Profits are increasing, and losses are piling up. If you can clarify to your satisfaction how the expenditure can contribute to increased revenue, do not be dissuaded by an expenditure that appears to be lossmaking. For instance, many people get caught up in the belief that they need the best possible Internet connection to ensure that their podcasts are downloaded lickety-split. That may be important at the point where some advertisers or paying listeners begin to complain that the connection is too slow but having more archival content available at slower speeds may be more important for success early in the life of a podcasting company because that is the formula for increasing the subscriber base. Similarly, by buying the costly microphone while forgoing a telephone recording interface, you will produce even less value because it will limit your opportunity to speak to in-studio guests. We can't tell you all the ways you can spend money, but we can tell you to look at your costs carefully from the very beginning. And, should an expenditure begin to prove to be unprofitable, such as having paid for too much bandwidth early on, don't be afraid to cut your losses by adjusting, even if it turns out that you don't really need to end a hosting arrangement or return the leased equipment. N In order to make profits, service providers exist. In information technology today, "outsourcing" is all the rage. Companies outsource hosting, almost all, of their websites, accounting systems, and services. That's fine, but for you, it can be cruel, too. The big purchasing option for most manufacturers in the podcasting world has to do with outsourcing hosting and programmed distribution. Hosting companies are in the money-making sector, so their expenses are protected and the homes of workers paid for, not to mention that investors at some point get a profit back. The truth of hosting is that you'll pay too much for something, whether it is bandwidth or storage. These businesses benefit from "breakage," the services for which they get consumers to pay, but they are not used. We think that storage is where you will be gouged most often since bandwidth is shared and prioritized among the hosting provider's customers to maximize the income of the host. In other terms, on the bandwidth side of the equation, a lot more breakage is available. Storage, on the other hand, is monopolized by the user-the hosting company that does not hold the data of two users in the same room, so that's where you're going to pay a premium for the space you use, also in the digital delivery environment after scarcity. Keep an eye out on what they actually charge for and what they are willing to give up maximizing your spending as you deal with these firms. N Partnering is another type of service payment. You may prefer to partner with another company that offers to manage a large part of your business for a share of revenue instead of choosing to pay for services, such as hosting and delivery bandwidth. These businesses, too, are trying to increase their profits, so in order to cut the best deal possible for you, you need to consider their costs as well as yours. Their initial offer is going to benefit them, regardless of how generous it might sound, so be prepared to haggle a little like anyone entering the bazaar. In order to understand where you can make a better deal, read the "window sticker" as you would on a new car. N This is your baby; feed it correctly. A company is like an infant. It always wants more for it or for you than it can be healthy. The assertion generally expresses this idea in business tomes that one must "be ruthless" about the use of funds and employee efficiency. Since many podcast companies start from the founder's outpouring of excitement and those who might be associated with it (like the engineer you brought in who wants to get some on-air time, or your uncle who loves the show and loves you more), it can be especially hard to live by the rules of ruthlessness. In these situations, sometimes, it helps to think a bit more like a caring mother. If you had a baby who, at 18 months of age, weighed 70 pounds, you would know the kid was eating something that wasn't right for his body. You'd cut the sugar out. The baby will be moaning, stamping his foot, calling for candy. You should stand your ground or be a miserable parent. The same happens with an organization that early on has family-like ties. As a parent, you need to make choices that the corporation may complain about. Be strong.

The first choices you make that affect your present and future costs have to do with bandwidth and storage space when you launch your podcast. Unlimited bandwidth, the ability of the network to deliver your display, will seem to be the main component of your costs, but it won't always be so. We advise you to choose a company that provides unlimited bandwidth because it is the aspect that will unexpectedly impact your costs: you cannot intend to have an unexpected hit that a million people instantly download, but if it does, unlimited bandwidth arrangements will prevent your podcast hosting bills from rising to tens of thousands of dollars. If possible, your first choice should be your long-term choice since moving a podcast from one server to another can take time, and it can cost you, listeners, if viewers lose track of your feed. Some hosting companies offer unbelievable offers that are not sustainable, just as you would suspect. Today, this is a less critical topic than ten years ago, when the Web first came along, and no one understood the requirements for choosing a trustworthy hosting company. However, if anyone tells you that if you only sign up for a year or two of service, you'll never pay more than $9.95 a month for hosting, be very careful. If they go out of business, the host will almost certainly not refund your money.

5.2 The Hosting Realities

Two items are supported by hosting providers: storage space, where you store your podcasts, and bandwidth, also known as "throughput," required for an audience to distribute your podcasts. They charge for both, though the combination of fees might highlight one or the other. Generally speaking, they want you to have as many shows on their server as possible if a hosting company provides unlimited storage so that you pay for plenty of downloads or, rather, for the bandwidth used by those downloads. Usually, these hosts offer bandwidth every month in blocks of megabytes or gigabytes. If the provider emphasizes free or limitless bandwidth, they usually charge for storage at fairly exorbitant rates to ensure that they are successful. When looking at launching a podcast, you should consider two basic types of hosting providers: the generic Web server host that is likely to charge based on a mix of storage and bandwidth used and a podcast host that offers podcast-specific services that are typically billed based on storage space. They each have strengths. If you just don't want to deal with setting up and handling audio streams, the podcast-specific hosts are great; they also save you from shouldering massive bandwidth costs if you have a hit show that unexpectedly takes off. On the other hand, it's more costly than you may think to store even a year's worth of podcasts with a host that gives you free bandwidth. You need a broad catalog to optimize the ability to win fresh subscribers, as we've described. The one thing is that, contrary to the iconic reputation of the medium as "free," podcasting needs substantial investment. Of course, several orders of magnitude are still cheaper than purchasing and running a radio station. Here, then, are some worksheets that will help you understand where each form of hosting deal will raise your costs.

Using your existing servers is one of the popular solutions for podcasters, which is a key idea if you can access loads of storage and bandwidth.

However, if you're going to surpass your current hosting cap, it could be as costly as outsourcing the hosting or more so. Both writers manage some of our own websites and are happy with having those files on servers running out of our home or collocation facilities with podcasts that attract hundreds of people. Believe it or not, you can possibly host your non-profit or small for-profit podcast from your house, even if you have a DSL or cable modem connection in your home that supports fixed IP addresses (which you use to host a server that can be found by people on the Internet).

5.3 Learning the Fundamentals

For most podcasters, hosting and distribution costs make up most of the expenditures, but when you create your first benefit and loss worksheet, there are other costs to take into account. You need to weigh the expense of office space and marketing materials if you are planning to start a podcast production company providing services to corporate customers. Often it takes office or at least a joint conference space you can use to host clients to make a good impression on customers. Your demo reel, written collateral, and a Web presence that sets the right tone are marketing expenses. Mad, trendy, or competent, the messaging needs to fit the consumer's expectations about their message's content and sound and be attractive. Service providers, as well as the total hosting costs, need to be analyzed from a project perspective. Your preparation must take into account how much time, materials, and ongoing costs are involved in producing the program when you take on a job, such as production for a local car dealership. If a customer plans to host the program himself, you can at least look over certain costs to ensure that his standards are compatible with what he is going to pay for. Often, just telling the customer that his expectations are in line with reality will win his confidence and provide the project with a more profitable and practical budget. But you should not start with a guess about the cost of the project and later seek to make up unforeseen losses; customers will keep you to the costs you initially quote. It is critically necessary for success in a service sector to have a transparent and comprehensive work plan for pricing that can change if the customer changes his orders later. Be prepared to lay out and clarify all the expected costs for yourself and the client before you begin every project so that you are not shocked by expenses or find yourself paying for the client's changing needs. You might be tempted to look at all the projects and think, "Hey, I do a lot on each project," but you forget the fixed costs you have to run your business. Everything needs to be included in the calculations: office, marketing expenses, accounting costs, billing costs. As a service provider, you can't ask one or two clients to do all this. And if you think of it as being offset by one or two projects' earnings, the fixed costs have to be split over the entire month. So, look at the number of hours involved in executing the contract when you prepare a project, and distribute your fixed costs over the whole month, break them, and include them in your hourly billing. Your profit margin will evaporate instantly if you do not take these costs into consideration. When you pay the cost of staying in the company, you'll just think you're making money. In these projected costs, everything has to be included. Very. Really. We've known so many producers who never really broke even because they saw projects as separate from their business, believing they were making good money. Too often, on the first project of the month, manufacturing firms try to charge all their costs and, as a result, lose business to rivals with more aggressive pricing. If you're not working on projects 40 hours a week, be prepared for most of the month, or all month, in the first year or two of the company, to lose money on certain core costs of doing business. Starting with a reasonable cost strategy, the pricing would stay competitive and give you an image of the organization that eliminates the unexpected surprises that startups often face when their strategies meet the realities of the industry.

5.4 Advertising Costs Money

Beyond the hosting fees, launching a commercial podcast has costs. The cost of reaching out to sponsors and marketers is real. If you search for ads yourself, the time you spend with family or friends comes out of it. It costs you out of your pocket every month if you hire someone to sell ads. Commission-only salespeople hold no "risk," but they typically sell lots of different items and opportunistically, so they might not spend much time on your program if they do well for anyone else. And once ad revenue comes through the gates, you won't really know if any sales work is being completed. There's the question of collecting it after the expense of identifying advertisements or sponsor sales. If you don't have a billing system in place, you just have to count the cost of issuing invoices as an expense. It is reasonably easy to pay for early and quick sponsorships since they could be focused on your work's general appreciation. A company may pay $500 a month for you to mention them as a sponsor. The problem is, when you seek premium fees and reach higher traffic levels that can be related to volume-based pricing, the ad/sponsor billing relationship needs more documentation.

For their money, advertisers want the most. You want the best for the role (admit it, you do). Documentation is the solution to your common predicament. You need to be able to show advertisers how many individuals download your podcast and/or listen to it. In magazine ads, the organization is audited by independent third parties who report on magazine circulation. Similarly, on the radio and TV. The early Web advertisement sector's early measurements of podcasting, focused on the number of downloads, are somewhat close to the estimation of audience size. But over the last decade, counting web pages has matured to a number of sophisticated metrics, all of which rely on turning viewers into consumers, beyond' clicks,' which may count various sections of a website as separate pages and inflate the outcomes. For instance, Google's AdSense programmed pays for actual clicks on ads, not the number of times an ad is seen. The calculation of ads will grow rapidly in podcasting over the next couple of years. We don't know all the ways it will grow, but it's definitely going to be more difficult to advertise than it is now.

There are chances that somebody might be injured if you invite people to your home or workplace for filming. Business visits may not cover the insurance on your house. You've got to search. You need to address the problem of insuring yourself against errors and omissions, the mistakes you can make while delivering services, or doing a commercial podcast that provides advice or information that listeners can act on. For instance, if you talk about investing, listeners can act on that data and lose money. Yeah, they do know the investment risks are there, but you gave them advice. And you make money or appear to be from your show's ads, so you might look like a lawsuit target. Insurers offer plans on accidents and omissions, also referred to as E&O insurance, that you might choose to buy. E&O insurance may be for you if you write your own scripts or commercials, provide services that consumers may challenge later (think about what happens if your promotional results turn out to be incorrect, for example), or make suggestions on risky subjects, such as health or investment. A publisher's exemption, however, covers journalists and commentators who warn against liabilities. Unfortunately, this was exploited by, for instance, stock analysts pumping stocks they owned. Suppose you need protection, whether for your home or accidents and omissions, we're not taking a stand. Instead, in order to ensure that you do not place your personal assets or income on the line because a listener wishes to sue you, it is something you need to take into your considerations and consult a professional-a lawyer, not an insurance salesman.

There isn't free podcasting. You need to consider a wide variety of costs that must be covered before you can hope to benefit, depending on the type of podcast or podcasting service you schedule. Even if it's just to find out how much an exciting hobby will cost you, begin by creating your podcasting profit and loss statement. You can cut costs in several ways, but they all have their own expenses. Making outsourcing and partnering decisions will cost you much too much in payments or revenue shared with partners without thoroughly knowing your business needs. Based on a combination of how much storage you need to keep all your archives online, note the long tail and the throughput needed to deliver your program to an audience that will sustain your expenses, make your hosting and delivery choices. N Start out slowly. No company, particularly show business, has instant achievements. Take into account all of the expenses, including supplies, marketing costs, and advertising costs. Find out how long you need to recover your investment and allocate those expenses to each display or project so that your clients, whether customers or advertisers, will spread them equally. Pricing must be competitive and equitable. N Occasionally, with good podcasters, bad things happen. When starting a company, speak to a lawyer, accountant, and other professionals that any businessperson might consult.

The first step toward generating value that you need to maintain and develop is to start a company. If your podcast uses popular music, your small media company needs to understand the rules of music licensing, and you need to know how to handle the risks associated with publishing knowledge and opinion so that you do not end up giving away any of the value you generate than required. For years, music has been a part of your recording experience. It is central to commercial broadcasts, and music has become a life-long fascination for the audiophile. A fake radio show made in your bedroom when you were a kid, using music for a mixtape, or if you are like us, is second nature because it was free and enjoyable. You make a copy for which the music industry needs to be charged when you use music for non-commercial programming, even if you didn't make anything for the transaction. Adding income makes the show a priority for music executives all the more enticing, and podcasts would definitely be at the core of some labels' business strategies as they rise in popularity. Know how to surf the fair use limits and when you should be prepared to pay, so you can make good choices about how much and when to use music. Some of the freedoms that journalists have enjoyed for decades are now earned by bloggers and podcasters, but they also need to be mindful of the laws on libel, slander, and defamation, all of which are facets of the same issue, openly damaging the reputation of someone. It's really a matter of keeping inside well-established lines, but a world of headaches can be avoided by understanding those lines.

5.5 Making Fair Use Feasible and Machine-Readable

In recent years, copyright has been expanded to extravagant lengths, and we've addressed the ramifications for podcasters and anyone who buys digital audio, video, and other media elsewhere. Without being a dick about it, you can get and use copyrights on your works. It can be useful to do so, as it allows you to have some control of what happens to your work while allowing others to quote you or sample audio or video within the limits you have defined. "Fair use" is a phrase bandied around these days since rights are in the center of too much transition due to the ease of copying and sampling the works of others. In the simplest terms, it grants an author the right to extract another work without permission in-depth articles on it. For instance, it is perfectly legal under U.S. copyright law to remove a quote or a paragraph from a book or play a short clip of a song or video so that you can criticize the material, something that can involve arguing with the job, not just doing a review. You may also make cash on the job that removes another work, such as when you sell a movie review or when a podcaster records a news story "quotes" from the audio. However, when it comes to making cash mainly from the excerpted work, there is a bright line. It is not fair to sell an audiobook or a film in the last 20 minutes so that people can find out how it ends. A teacher can distribute a copy of an article for class discussion, but in the digital age, the boundaries are so limited that almost any copying is regarded by some industries, particularly the music industry and Hollywood, as a breach of copyright, although the typical software company would not be kind to anyone who copies part of its source code, even for educational purposes. There are few saints left in this world, so try to join the team on this subject with the white hats; be very liberal in your thoughts about fair use but be vigilant and respectful of others' intellectual property because you may be sued for errors. An attorney and Stanford Law School professor, Lawrence

Lessig, conceived of a copyright supplement that reflects an author's ambitions for her work while maintaining a broad form of fair use. The scheme, called Creative Commons, depends on a license that allows individuals, as long as they give you credit, to make copies and redistribute all or parts of your work with or without adjustments. If you don't make any commercial use, it restricts people from reselling or profiting from your work. As machine-readable explanations of the rights, you give to others, Creative Commons licenses are designed to be embedded in works. This is important for potential intellectual property systems implementations, but it is not supported today in digital media players, so it does not mean that your licensed Creative Commons software is protected from unauthorized copying. It's not DRM; it's just a form of metadata that travels to streamline the re-use of sound or photos for your podcast. The important principle behind Creative Commons is that society is interested in media conversations and debates, so the freedom to relate to and change other works while engaging in these discussions is vital to an open and informed society that thrives on exchanging ideas sales. Making your plans readily available encourages individuals to use your job without first having to consult with you, but it doesn't mean that all other doors have been locked. So, if you do not want your Creative Commons license to be used commercially, anyone who wants to republish it for commercial purposes must contact you to negotiate a price. Your contact information is carried by the Creative Commons license so that individuals can talk with commercial uses you. With Creative Commons, you will need to register any job you want to protect, which means that you can protect all your podcasts under one license. However, if you want to create various programmers or handle various programmers differently, you need to create a license for each of them.

Music brings emotional energy to every show and listeners who are used to hearing music that supports what the host is saying view a podcast without music as sparse. The problem is, when you try to redistribute it, popular music costs money, even as a background sound in a podcast.

5.6 Licensing

Music brings emotional energy to every show and listeners who are used to hearing music that supports what the host is saying view a podcast without music as sparse. The problem is, when you try to redistribute it, popular music costs money, even as a background sound in a podcast.

As a general rule, podcasters create material that is likely to be appealing to only a small group of listeners. Podcasts begin with an idea, something you have the desire and expertise to speak about, either actual or imaginary. Add a bit of motivation to that, a do-it-yourself, and an inability to take no for an answer. The aim is to tell those who would like to hear what you want to learn. Podcasts can be about anything, and just about anyone can appreciate them. The subjects mentioned do not need to be earth-shattering or life changing. You have a handful of rules to obey, but even then, you can break the majority of them. Some of the most popular podcasts are made by ordinary individuals who sit a few nights a week in front of their computers and just talk about their minds, hearts, and souls. Some concentrate on niche subjects; some are more broad-based. Apparently, quite a few were put together at random, perhaps moments before the recording began.

I've heard more than one complaint from a podcaster about the fact that they get, well, well, Remarks. Feedback. Podcast listeners are more likely to have input on the shows they listen to for some explanation (which we will let the social anthropologists of the future puzzle out) than radio show listeners are likely to e-mail their thoughts to the show host. The personal essence of choosing a podcast is possibly traceable to that. Podcasts provide more access, choices, and intimacy to their listeners and creators than conventional broadcast media would. Of course, the radio is much harder to talk to than a machine with an Internet connection and an e-mail address (which remains the killer app). You are likely to get it and from unexpected locations when you ask for input. Since geography does not restrict the distance your podcast can travel, you can find yourself in faraway and exotic places with listeners. And this feedback is not going to always be "Wow, great podcast!" "When you're welcome reviews, listeners will be frank with you. Nice, if you're beginning to get the impression that podcasting is innovative, groundbreaking, and maybe a major component of social upheaval. Not all podcasts are that deep, however. Many of them, in truth, is just plain fun.

Chapter 6: Money Making with Podcasting

Your podcast is going to be up and running before too long. You will have a science-based development process, your content will be concentrated and motivated, and your audience will expand at a good, steady pace. There's nothing like the days of the youth of your podcast, watching what was recently a mere idea grow into a continuing, full-fledged concern. Now you are busy with your new offspring, reviewing download stats, replying to e-mails, and thinking about your favorite podcast directory ranking. "When your show is a bit mature, and you have gained some exposure as a podcaster, you're going to start wondering, "What's next? The show is going well, and your viewers are getting great answers, but in what ways can you expand the show and mobilize your newfound audience? Your mind, like many before you, could turn to money, dare we say it. Many podcast purists strongly believe (especially from the early days) that podcasting is an art form and that a person should create a podcast for his or her own sake. Bravo to someone so selfless because it is hard work to do podcasting. Preparing is hard work, recording/editing/mastering is hard work, and its hard work to encode and update blog posts. Yeah, maybe it's not hard work, but it's still a lot of work. Why not get paid for it because podcasting is work? There has been a great deal of discussion about podcasting "monetizing."

Monetizing, obviously, is a business term for "turning it into a company." Fair enough. From moments after its inception, people have been fretting about how to monetize this new medium. Why all the fretting, then? For decades, the tried-and-true business models that have served radio, TV, and independent artists can easily be borrowed from podcasters. Now, if you have an advertisement sales team in your basement, you're probably pretty straightforward about how you could market your podcast for some time. But we'll start slowly with a few easy ways for everyone else to raise, well, maybe not millions, but at least enough money to cover your expenses.

6.1 Make Money from The Media

Let's be very transparent about how making money in the media works before we get into the details of how to monetize your podcast (since that's what we're actually doing here). Not to be too frank about it, but you need to get someone to give you his or her money in order to make money. Easy, huh? Ok, exactly how are you going to do that? You're exploiting an audience. Your audience, bar none, is your greatest asset. It's just you and a mic and some recording equipment without your audience. Your audience is one hundred or one hundred thousand people who regularly sign up for your show. Whether through e-mailing feedback, phoning you, or simply downloading your broadcast, they actively engage in your podcast. So, how are you going to use the audience to make money? Give something to the audience that they'd pay money for. Give your audience to someone who is dying to pay for them as a target group. As evidence that you know how to attract and develop an audience, sell your audience to companies, and employ yourself as a podcast producer. Throughout this chapter, we'll address these points. We'll start by covering areas you can learn about your audience, which is the foundation for any next steps you take in marketing and advertising.

It can seem difficult at first to pinpoint precisely what the audience is willing to pay for. Fortunately for us, it simply doesn't take much time to figure it out. Setting up donation ties or providing a range of products that once have required a significant upfront investment in time and resources. These days, we can set up online transactions in no time, thanks largely to the Internet. Ask yourself, considering who you think they are, what kind of "stuff" your audience would want. At a fair price, can you think of anything to sell that they would really like and enjoy and that is a natural extension of your podcast? Or would it suffice to deliver the podcast itself?

6.2 Contributions and Subscriptions

It is something for which you may have mixed feelings to go straight to your subscribers for donations or membership fees. Asking for cash is something certain individuals really aren't comfortable with. However, the situation's flip side is that your audience will be more than willing to contribute to subsidizing the show. Your audience may be able to share a bit of your new financial burden, whether it is to feel more connected to the podcast, show their gratitude, or just help prevent you from having to search for sponsors.

6.3 Promotion as a tool

It's time to gain some attention after all the time, resources, and expenditure you put into your podcast. Speak about business models all you want, but your audience delivers the coin; without an audience, you have no business model regardless of the business model. You're not going to find a "Build It, And They're Coming" model. Before you can make things work, you have to constantly recruit and retain the attention of people. Fortunately, where podcasts are mentioned and discussed, hundreds of sites operate. Your marketing's keystone is putting your podcast on those platforms and encouraging listeners to chat about your show with social tags and other group structures, so your listeners are really in control of the outcome. You should only get the conversation started, so get people talking.

For any form of business, the two basic pieces of the puzzle are promotion and passion. A passion for success and information about the client is required for every successful organization. You got that, or you wouldn't be reading about how to turn this dream into a business. Promotion is altogether another matter. The ability to attract publicity is gifted to certain individuals. For a variety of reasons, you need to think about how to create a brand for yourself. The brand is the experience that the listener takes away from any interaction with your podcast, specifically, the qualities remembered, such as "funny" or "honest" or "profitable." It is a representation of who you present yourself as or who you are, and it offers continuity and credibility if approached as a collection of principles for what you offer and provides a decision-making instrument when solving problems.